How To Anime

MW01170455

A Step by Step Guide

Printed in the United States of America
9798686574236

INSTRUCTIONS

Here you will find the basic steps necessary to replicate the figures found throughout this book.

1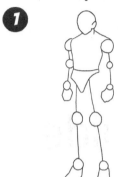

Every figure starts out with a basic outline.

2

The second step is where we flesh out the outline and give it a full form.

3

The third step we begin to add the first set of details such as hair and clothing.

4

In the fourth step we continue adding details and erasing lines that are no longer necessary.

5

Finally, in the fifth step we add the shading to select areas on the figure to give it depth.

GRAPHING PAPER

OPPOSITE EACH GUIDE YOU WILL FIND A BLANK SHEET OF OF 4X4 GRAPH PAPER. BY FOCUSING IN ON THE GRIDS YOU CAN BETTER PINPOINT AND EMULATE THE ART FEATURED IN THE GUIDES.

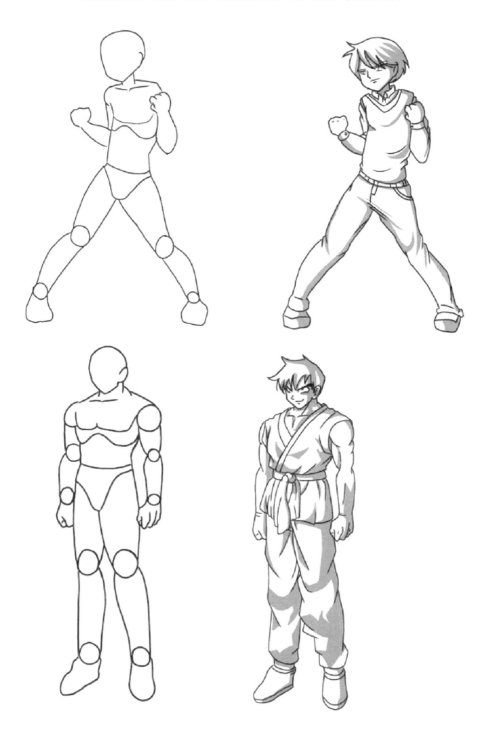

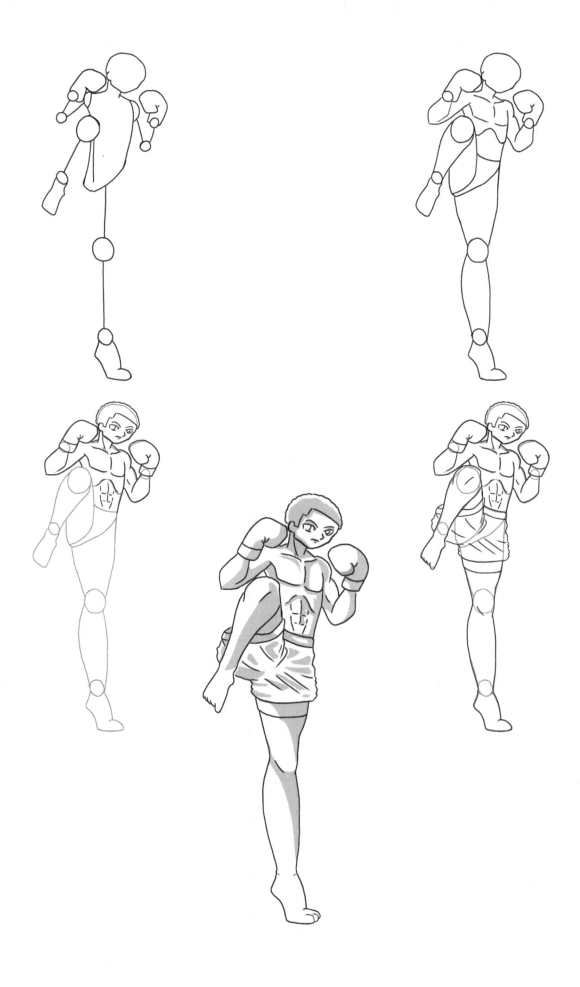

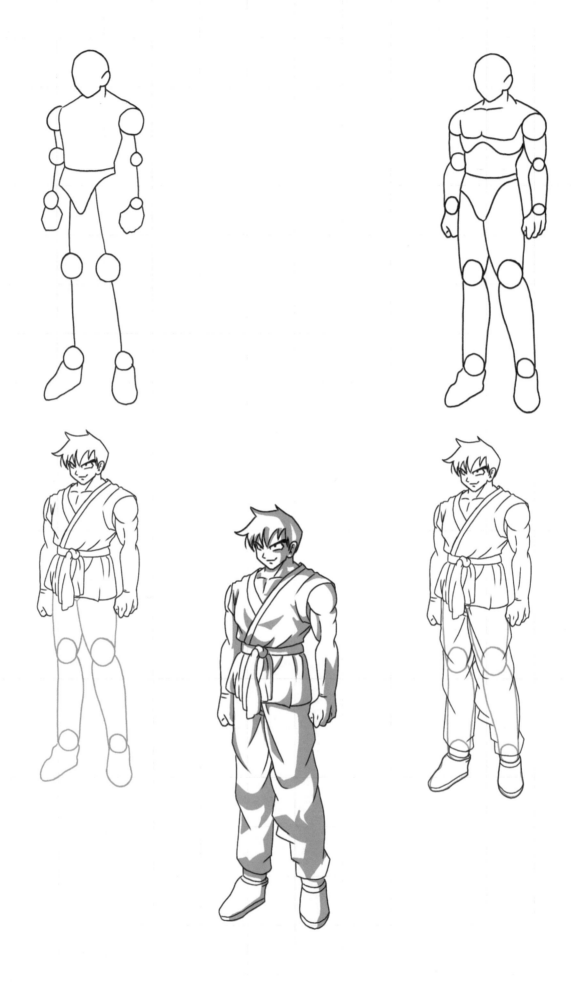

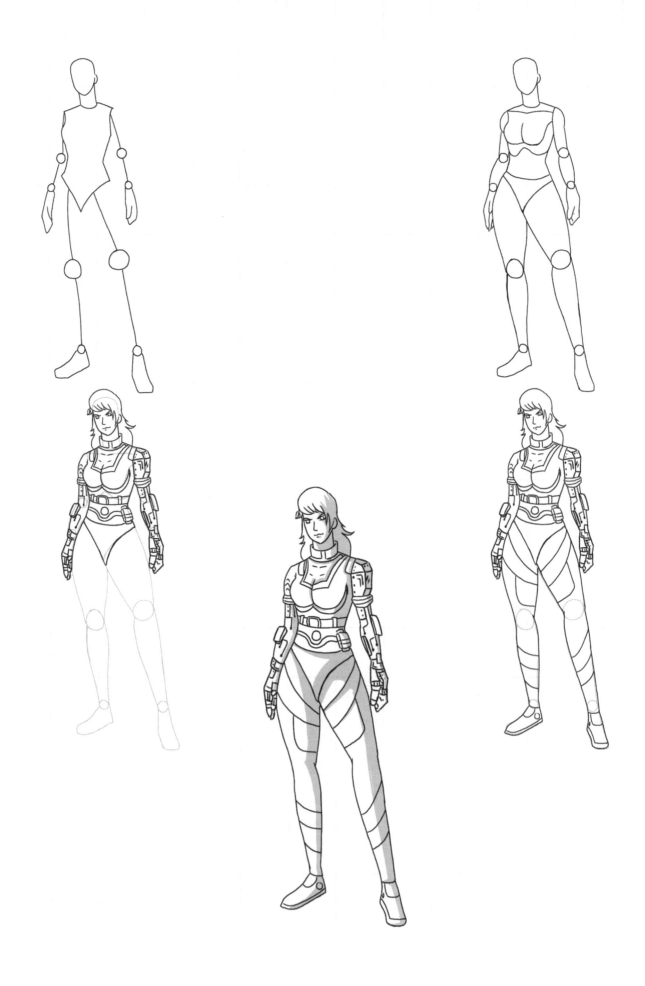

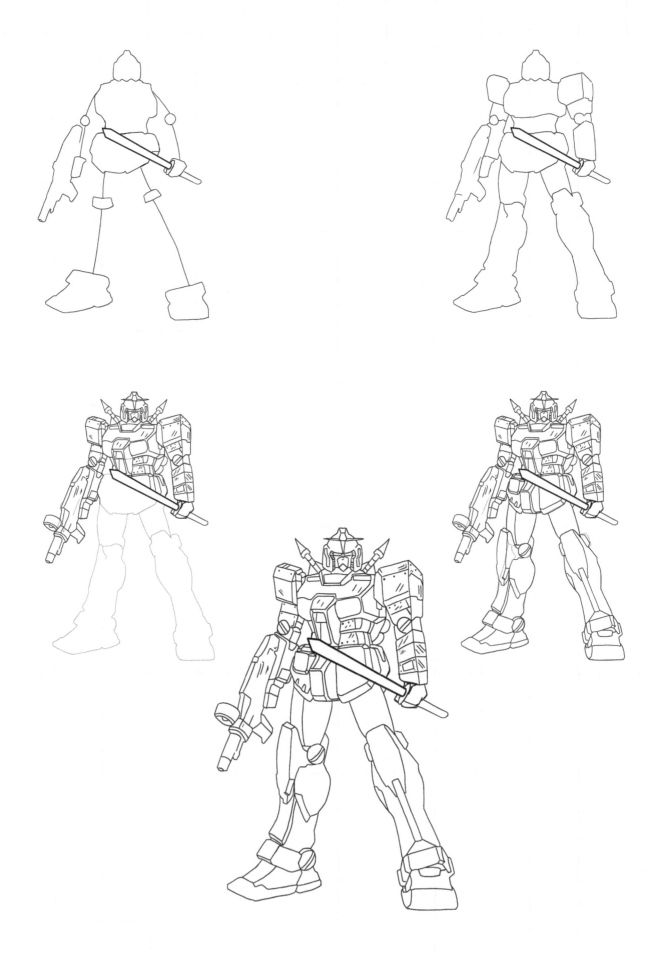

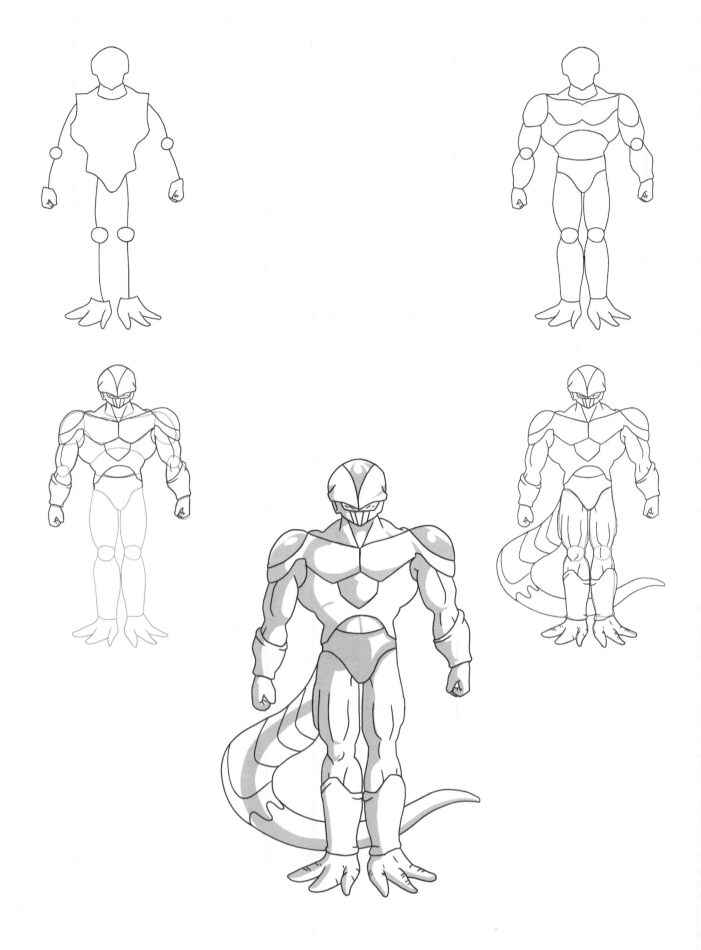

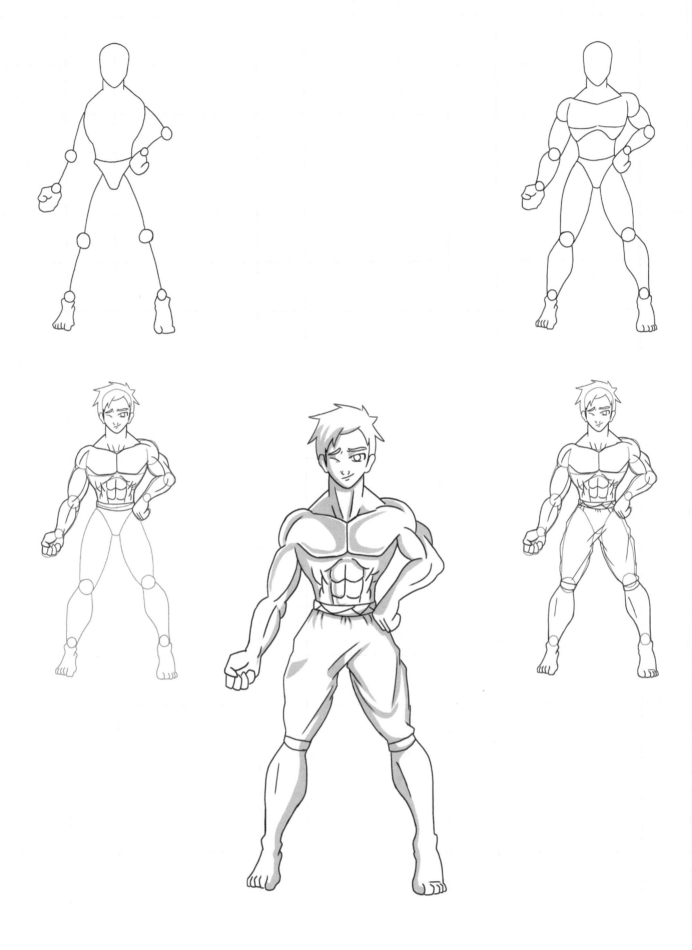

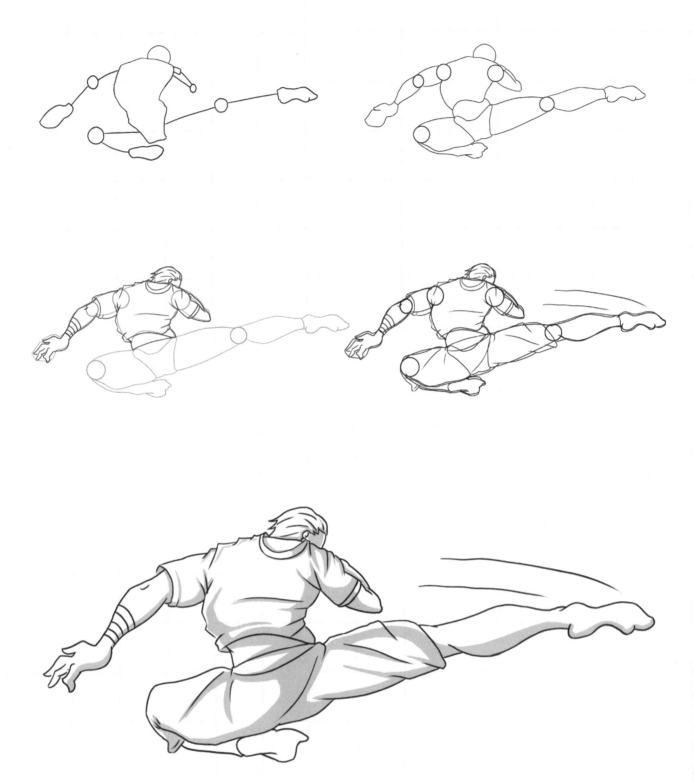

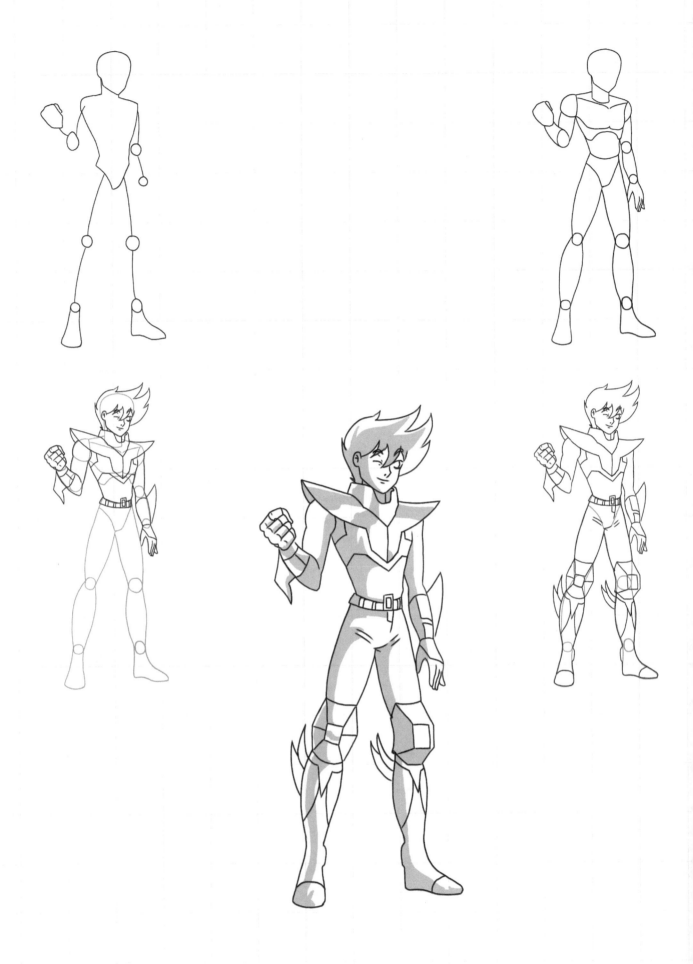

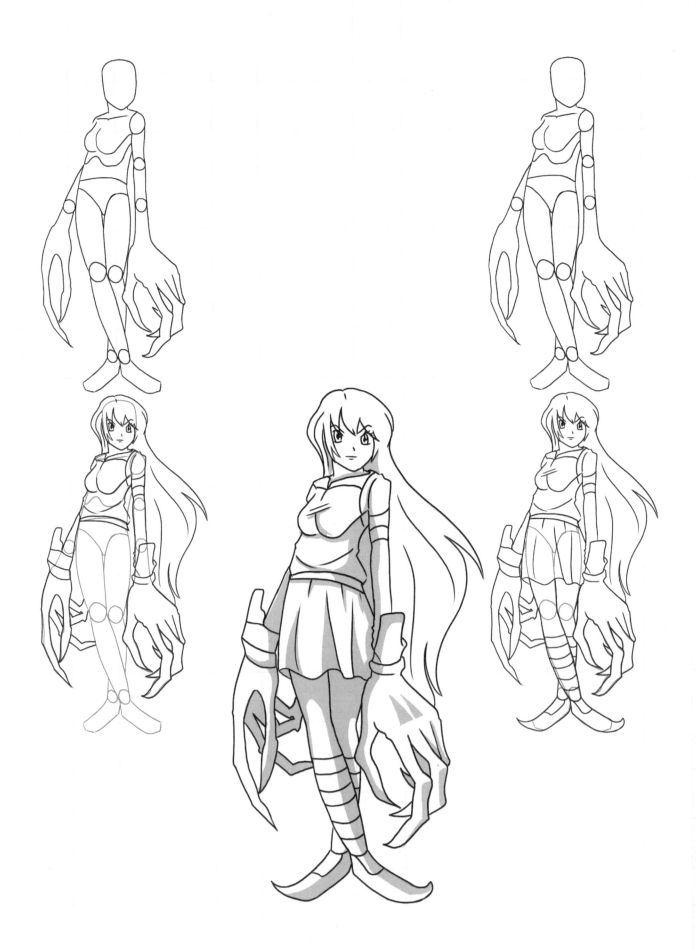

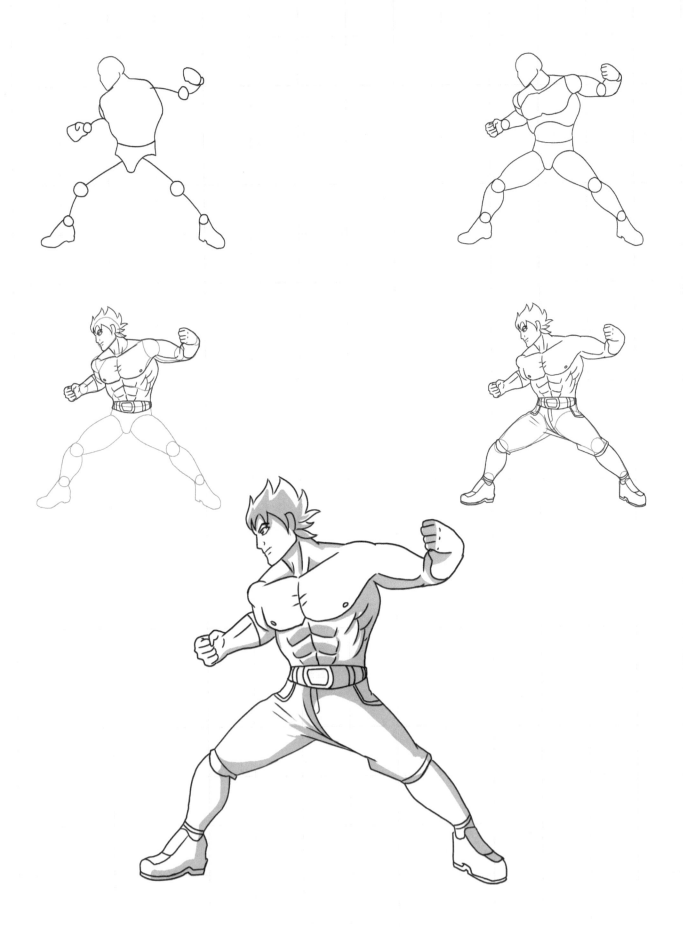

THANK YOU FOR YOUR PURCHASE!

We greatly appreciate your support. Without you, none of this would be possible. Please consider leaving us a review on Amazon.

Reviews greatly help us to be able to continue to produce books such as this one. Also, feel free to follow us on our social media channels or contact us directly at sketchpert.press@gmail.com

And be sure to join our exclusive Facebook Group for freebies, giveaways, and early preview copies!

@sketchperts

@sketchperts

Made in United States
Troutdale, OR
05/13/2025

31326726R00058